For Anne
with Love
Stephen Morris
Sept 76

DEATH OF A CLOWN

Other books by Stephen Morris include

The Lord of Death

Born under Leo

The Revolutionary

The Kingfisher Catcher

DEATH OF A CLOWN

STEPHEN MORRIS

aquila poetry

ACKNOWLEDGEMENTS

are due to the editors of the following publications in which some of the poems have appeared:—
POETRY WALES; THE BIRMINGHAM MAIL; TIME OUT; THE LITTLE WORD MACHINE; THE DAILY MIRROR; THE S'B' GAZETTE; THE NEW SOUTH and BRUSHFIRE.

ISBN O 7275 0114 3 CASED
ISBN O 7275 0115 1 CASED SIGNED
ISBN O 7275 0116 X PAPERBACK

Published by
The Aquila Publishing Co. Ltd.
9 Scullamus, Breakish, Isle of Skye, Scotland. IV42 8QB

CONTENTS

FOR CLAUDIA

TORSCHLUSSPANIC

(The panic of closing doors)

Well its here, and past.
Lost days, lost opportunities,
With the children growing up now
And my best friend
Promoted yet again.
Frustration nibbles at my conscience,
Stairs are harder to climb,
There are the difficult white hairs
And all the songs seem out of tune.
The options have suddenly disappeared
Leaving a world of younger men.
Everything is no longer possible,
The doors are all closing.
An old photograph tells all —
We did dress in a strange way then,
I wonder what happened to......
The film star, I loved so passionately,
What was her name again ?
The choice is limiting,
The doors are all closing,
And all the songs are out of tune.

CASUAL MEETING

Casually meeting her along the beach
I felt the years between us drain away,
Making the brief encounter as meaningful
As the stones which lay beneath our feet.
It was however, an unhappy contact,
For we talked in defensive trivia
Mentioning briefly our children,
Past acquaintances and the lost revolutions.
As we smiled reflectively at one another
We exchanged forbidden telephone numbers;
Promised faithfully to call one another
Then crunched our separate ways,
Thinking how old the other had become
But enjoying the security of it all.

GEISHA

HARAKIRI

KARATE

HIROSHIMA

FILM FAN

(For Elisha Cook Jr.)

By the second reel
I feel
That I could destroy
Without a trace
The face
Of Elisha Cook
And his miserable look.
The mournful
The all forlornful
The downright awful
That is Elisha Cook
And his miserable look.
I could run amok
With the cowardly crook,
I could thrash him
I could smash him,
I could desecrate
And annihilate
Liquidate
And suffocate
Emasculate
And mutilate
The face of Elisha Cook
With his miserable look.
Yes, I know that
I could really destroy
With considerable joy
Little old Elisha Cook
And his miserable look.

BUSBY BERKELEY POEM

SO THIS IS IMMORTALITY ?

So this is immortality ?
One wooden cross
With painted letters
Planted in an unwanted churchyard
In an unwanting town
How many times have you turned
In your lead-lined tomb
As the lips have moved
Whispering their odious curses ?
This town you have famed
This churchyard swamped by Americans
So this is immortality ?
One wooden cross
With painted letters.

(Written Laugharne July 1968)

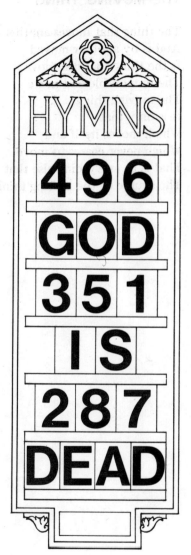

THE MOVING THING

The thing that moves another
And is by another moved
Is the thing that can move
The immovable and move
The moving thing
It is only that
Which moves itself and
Which never ceases to move
That is to everything else that moves
The source of the moving thing.

PENNY FARTHING MADNESS

It was penny farthing madness
The way you looked at me
With a wisp of hair on one side
A bow of red on the other
My heart holds a corner of sadness
My love for you had died
But the way you looked me over
My heart leaped up and cried
It was penny farthing madness
On that dark November day
You came like a morning hunter
You came to take your prey
You used your lips like razors
Your eyes were used like wine
You clung to my body till midnight
But no longer were you mine
It was penny farthing madness
On that dark November day
You left me for a season
When my feet had turned to clay.

A LOVE POEM

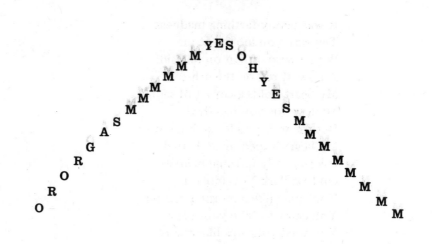

BED POEM

BODIES

Weightless bodies
spaceless
moving bodies
together in motion
floating bodies
moist
twisting bodies
joined
melting bodies
giving

bodies in desire
rushing
reaching bodies
thrusting
gripping bodies
in climax together

bodies exhausted
damp
bodies parting
bodies

LAUNDRETTE LOVE

The man sat in the laundrette
Smoking a cigarette
When he noticed a girl
Watching the whirl
Of the laundrette machine
Under the fluorescent lit sky
They were suddenly high
So he inserted his coin
And turned his key
The two became one
Which later became three.

LOVE 69? POEM

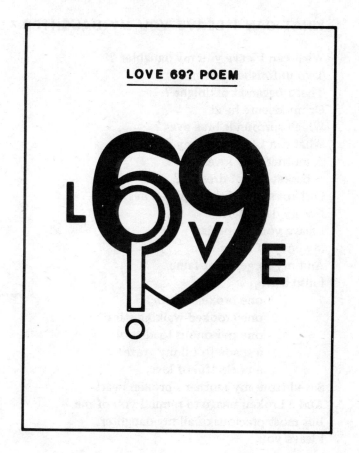

WHAT CAN I LEAVE YOU MY DAUGHTER ?

What can I leave you my daughter ?
Two unfinished poems
That I began at midnight ?
Or my square head
Which surrounds blue eyes ?
What can I leave you my daughter ?
A mother who loves you ?
A basket full of dreams ?
Perhaps a bookful of unlived lies ?
No my daughter.
I leave you my pride
My envy of other men
And my forgeries of fame.
I also leave,
        one broken mirror
        one crooked walking stick
        one poisonous toadstool
        a spade to fill my grave
        a pocketful of love
Saved from my mother's broken heart
And a broken image to remind you of me.
But most precious of all my daughter,
I leave you.

CONVERSATIONAL PIECE

As we were talking to one another
I realised that I was suddenly alone,
No beliefs and full of lost ideals.
A sorry figure one could accuse,
But I became at peace with myself
And that significantly was very important.
The debate,as always a futile one,
Continued aimlessly without reason,
Causing me to wish the talking would cease,
Eventually, they demanded responses to their words
But my mind, hypnotised in thought,begged only solitude,
Which choked my only comments with indifference.
The unforgivable was to be unforgotten
As all loquacious friends became my silent enemies.

APOLOGIES

It was when the shadows fell around
That you stared into my tired eyes,
As if reading words in my dark mind
Spelling out the same old lies.
Your self doubts were reflected
Carving rejection across your face,
Twisting me into a dangerous stranger
Eating out your heart in a heartless place.
The apologies they come easy
But the memories of love are marred,
For the seeds of hate they germinate
And forgiveness is much too hard.
It was when the shadows slowly darkened
That a new light slipped over me,
The girl with navy blue eyes forgotten
There are cucumber sandwiches for tea.

OLD MAN AMOK

The old man who lived in Sunset Terrace,
Which is situated London North-West one,
Was not only old but very jealous
So he bought a second-hand Luger gun.
With it he shot the young, the rich, anyone.
He shot a man, a girl, the Milkman too,
His wife, the Butcher and his eldest son.
A Policeman came to look for a clue
So the old man shot him in London North-West two.

DEAF AND DUMB POEM

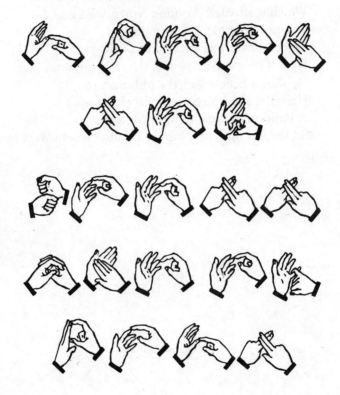

DEATH OF A CLOWN

This poem is about a man who was suffering from a severe depression. He went to a doctor and said, "Doctor, I'm so unhappy that I want to die." The Doctor, who considered himself to be something of a psychiatrist said, "What you need is something to snap yourself out of it. Why don't you go to the circus tonight and see the famous clown Grimaldi, he is the funniest man alive. He will cure you. The man looked sadly at the Doctor and said, "There's one thing that you don't understand Doctor, I am Grimaldi."

Grimaldi, Grimaldi
The sad faced clown
He had the saddest face
In the saddest town.
He made people laugh
He made them sing
Even in November
It was just like Spring.

A red bowler hat
A bright bow tie,
Baggy trousers
And a funny eye.

Grimaldi, Grimaldi
He was so sad
But when people saw him
It made them so glad.
He tumbled and he rolled
He turned upside down
The people didn't know
He was the sad faced clown.

He danced around
He did a pirouette,
He did a waltz
With his silhouette.

Grimaldi, Grimaldi
Went to work every day
Everyone loved him
But his work was just play.
He jumped and he joked
He was the funniest clown
But he was no more
Than a King with no crown.

Two big feet
A grinning face,
Falling around
With gentle grace.

Grimaldi, Grimaldi
He wanted to die
He was so unhappy
But he didn't know why.
They buried him alone
In a long white gown
Then everyone missed
The unhappy clown.

Grimaldi, Grimaldi
The sad faced clown
He had the saddest face
In the saddest town.
He made people laugh
He made them sing
Even in November
It was just like Spring.

SEMAPHORE POEM

SUNDAY MORNING MOODS

Sunday morning moods
Brought tensions to my mind.
It wasn't that I couldn't stand
The accusations, the jibes or the demands.
It wasn't even the futile debates on sex,
But it was the damn banging of make-up jars
And the pauses between thought and words.
The moods were sometimes black
But mostly they were pale grey or off white.
Some were dirty pink, but whatever their colour,
They inflicted everyone with their pigments.
These were the Sunday morning moods,
Monday mornings were a different story.

TO DESTROY THE FLAME

It's so cold
So cold and unreal
To sit waiting
And waiting
To take away the object
Of what was, and is
A part of you . . . . .
And me.
This form that lives
Deep within your body
A symbol
Which we are paying
The old fat woman
To murder.
Would that living mite
Which is protected
In your body
Request the fate
Such as we have decided
In our cold respectable
Logic ?
Would it, I wonder
Prefer
The early morning sun
And the warmth
Of its own body
Close to another
As we once were ?

I sit waiting
Clasping your cold hand
Waiting for that woman
To destroy the flame

ANNIVERSARY

Now after five furious years
I turn towards your blue eyes
To seek confirmation that you
Still love me tonight and every night
Now after sixty stormy months
I turn towards your smiling lips
To seek confirmation that I
Can have your eager kisses at midnight
Now after 1,826 desperate days
I turn towards your warm body
To seek confirmation that I
Can still arouse you on any night.

BALLAD FOR A YOUNG GIRL

Look into starlit darkness
Open an unlocked door
Walk up a marbled staircase
Don't take your eyes from the floor.

Wander alone through midnight caverns
Wish every time you cry
Ride an old iron horse on Monday
Kiss gravestones before you die.

Wear a flower when the sun shines
Place your hand in mine
Touch my body on Thursdays
But never drink sweet wine.

Walk through a blind man's garden
Measure your life in spoons
Shake hands with a lonely beggar
But never chase red balloons.

Wash your hands in raindrops
Swim under unfaithful skies
Drink from an empty wineglass
Believe in all my lies.

Tiptoe across silent Sundays
Bathe your breasts in a stream
Whisper aloud to your lover
Smoke to float on a dream.

Wink at a child with a lollipop
Hug every willow tree
Never give coins to a collector
Fly kites across the sea.

Sip sherry before your seduction
Light candles when we dine
Come very close for protection
Warm your body with mine.

Caress a Summer bluebell
Ride on an endless wind
Pick a flower for Jupiter
Make love all through Spring.

If you conceive on Friday
Go home without a word
Have my child on a Wednesday
And I'll tell all the world.

PARIS
IN THE
THE SPRING
PARIS IN THE
THE SPRING PARIS
IN THE SPRING

HAIKU

Lunchtime at Christmas
Family histrionics
Goodwill to all men.

Sir Winston Churchill,
The saviour of the British.
Bombs over Dresden.

The great French leader,
Napoleon Bonaparte.
Born under Leo.

The undertaker
Knew the price of everything,
But valued nothing.

LOVE HAIKU

Amsterdam meeting,
Love flows along the canals
Tulips for my girl.

The rhythm of Spring
Ebbing and flowing in love,
Hypnotised her mind.

The young girls dancing
Moving their vibrant bodies
Waiting for their men.

Picking new flowers
For Elizabeth and Jane.
Which one shall I choose ?

CLASSIFIED ADS
(Engagements, Marriages, Births & Deaths)

CATCHES

Alan and Dawn
Are to be wed
They made a mistake
When sharing her bed

MATCHES

Alan and Dawn
Conceived a mystery
The vicar didn't know
He was marrying three

HATCHES

To Alan and Dawn
For all their sins
Have given birth
To very fine twins

DESPATCHES

For the twins and Dawn
It's all very sad
Alan got killed
And now the twins have no Dad.

SKY HIGH

If Jesus was really hung up
And Saint Stephen was really stoned
God could be in a fix.

TO MY GIRL AT THE BANK

Last night with you
I withdrew.
Today, you I ignore
And overdraw.

HIPPIE POEM

DR P OUT

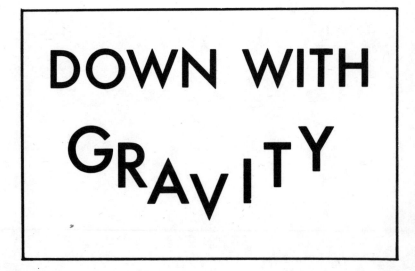

DOWN WITH GRAVITY

D AND O

Add a 'd' to evil
Subtract an 'o' from good
The evil now reads devil
And the good should now read God.

D and O
Dando
Dan do
O nadd
And do
Nad do
Do dan
Do and
Odd an
Ad don
And do
D noad
Nod da
Dan do
Na dod
No dad
Nod ad
An odd
Do nad
Dad no
And do
Dando
D and O

Subtract a 'd' from devil
Add an 'o' to God
The devil should now read evil
And the God should now be good.

YESTERDAY'S GIRL

Yesterday's girl
Lies unconvincingly
Across from me,
Her smiles
Taste of revenge,
But she is beautiful.

Her eyes
Full of accusations
And pain,
Reflect my face
Which is covered
In false excuses.

Yesterday's girl,
Her body
Full of promises
Invites me
To share her tomorrow
As well as our today.

Yesterday's girl
With touches
Of silk
Suddenly forgets
All the days,
And she is beautiful.

SHE CAME, THE SAME

Twice a day she came,
The same
Face, nose freckled, blue eyed,
Smiled
Hello and whispered a wish
Formed as a kiss.
Twice a day she went,
Spent
Of love and lust.
In trust
She returned,
Spurned, to another.

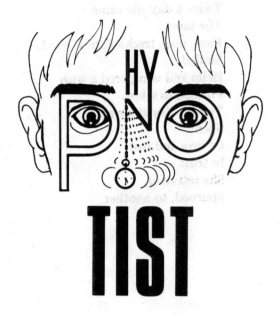

THE DARK GIRL

The dark girl
Hidden in hair beauty
Danced her love,
Moving gently
As she floated
Her kisses
Over my body.
She wanted
Neither sun, nor rain, nor wind,
Only the touch of me.

No false moments here,
For her tears
Fell like raindrops
Across my chest,
Surrounding my heart
With a tenderness.
There we lay, as innocent
As children
Drifting like soft clouds
Across the night.

At dawn,
The warm dark body
Cooled with regrets,
Slipping out of reach
With thoughts of others
And loss.
She wanted
Only the sun, the rain and the wind.
She wanted anything,
Anything, but the touch of me.

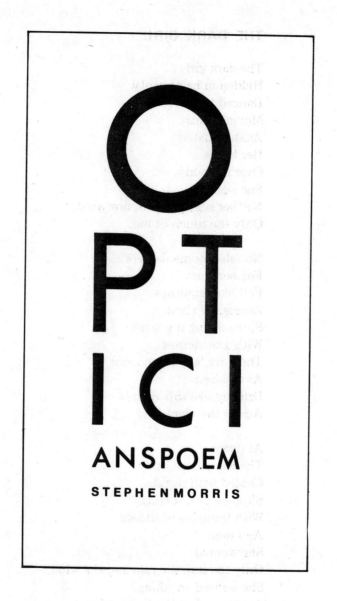

COUNTING

I muse in the marital bliss
Pausing to wonder what's amiss.
Wondering why the magic
Has slipped away — rather tragic.

Remember the early morning kisses
The flowers and cheap red wine ?
The white sheets and wishes
And telling each other, you'll always be mine ?

We would pause, I remember
Even then, to count the leaves,
Or blades of grass, but now we count
The children leaving home — alas.

PHASING OUT

The pain was in evidence;
During the last chilling days,
Revealed in her twig fingers
Which clawed out in wild defence,
As if reaching for monsters
That lurked in a painful maze.

The burning flame blazed briefly;
Flickered then quietly died,
The ring of people parted
Revealing the naked bride,
Lost now to all the worldly
And joining the painless dead.

KITCHENER POEM

YOUR COUNTRY NEEDS
YOU
SO GO ON HOME AND
WRITE A POEM